NEEDLEPOINT

NEEDLEPOINT

HILARY MORE
SERIES EDITOR: ROSEMARY WILKINSON

SUNBURST BOOKS

Note: Imperial and metric measurements are not direct equivalents, so always follow only one set in a particular method.

This edition first published in 1994 by
Sunburst Books, Deacon House, 65 Old Church Street,
London, SW3 5BS

Created and produced by
Rosemary Wilkinson and Malcolm Saunders Publishing Ltd
4 Lonsdale Square, London N1 1EN

ISBN 1 85778 045 0

Printed and bound in Hong Kong

Illustrations: Kate Simunek, Terry Evans
Design: Ming Cheung
Cover photograph: by courtesy of Paterna Yarns, P O Box 1,
Ossett, West Yorkshire WF5 9SA

Contents

Introduction

Needlepoint is the sturdiest form of embroidery: it's worked with a needle and yarn onto a base of strong canvas or evenweave fabric. The stitches used in this craft have been devised over the years, not only as a form of decoration but also to reinforce the canvas base in order to make it suitable for all types of home furnishings.

The earliest, and most commonly-used stitches today, are tent stitch and cross stitch. The yarns that can be used range from the traditional wools to cotton, silk and metallic threads.

In addition to providing guidance on creating traditional needlepoint pieces for cushions and pictures, the methods shown in this book will lead you to experiment with more adventurous fabrics, patterns and stitches. These can be used to create a variety of things for the home, as well as belts, hat bands and other pieces of decorative embroidery to enhance plain items of clothing.

This book will provide you with an instant reference for needlepoint techniques and presents clear instructions and diagrams for all the stitches you need to create beautiful and original pieces of canvaswork.

Part 1:
EQUIPMENT

Canvas

Any material with an even grid of threads can be used for needlepoint but canvas is specifically made for this type of embroidery. Natural canvas is a fairly stiff, open, evenweave fabric constructed in cotton or linen in white, beige or cream. Plastic canvas is now also available (see below). White canvas makes the best background against which to distinguish yarn colours but can be tiring for the eyes when stitching intricate work. Beige can be too dark a ground for pastel yarns.

Canvas size

Canvas is graded by the number of threads or holes to the inch (centimetre).   This is called the mesh size and is usually described as a number followed by "hpi". For example, a mesh size of 12hpi means that the canvas has twelve threads or holes per inch (2.5cm).

There is a wide variety of canvas sizes from a very fine 30hpi to the most open rug canvas at 3hpi. Canvases with 16hpi or more are described as "petit point" and those with fewer than 16hpi are termed "gros point".

Canvas types

There are different qualities to choose from and, as with other fabric, when you choose a good quality, you gain a good result. There are two main types of canvas: single and double thread. When buying a piece of canvas, check that it is free from flaws and knots.

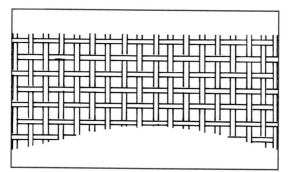

Single or mono canvas is woven with single threads horizontally and vertically. The size is determined by the number of holes or threads per inch (centimetre).

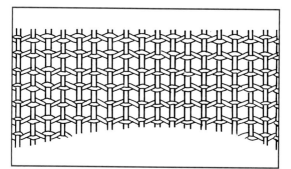

In the better quality canvas the threads are woven through each other and this type is called **interlocked**. Single canvas is easier to use especially for a beginner, as any stitch can be worked over the even-gridded surface.

Double or Penelope canvas has pairs of threads interwoven horizontally and vertically. As the threads are double this type is often counted by the number of holes rather than threads. The double

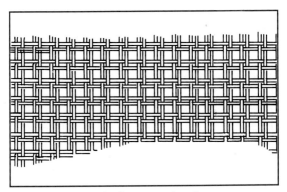

threads can be pushed apart so that the canvas can be used as though it were a single canvas. This will produce smaller stitches creating smoother curved lines and therefore is used for areas of fine work, such as facial features or fine details on floral or animal designs. When the work needs to be trammed or padded (see page 69), double canvas is easier to use than single, as the trammed stitches can be worked between the pairs of threads.

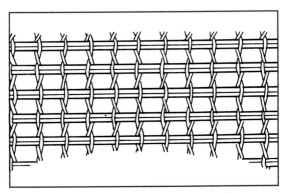

Rug canvas is a coarse double canvas with 3, 5 or 7 holes to the inch (2.5cm).

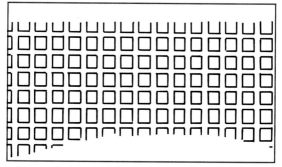

Plastic canvas is the new arrival on the market. Composed of a transparent, rigid mesh, this type of canvas is bought in squares and rectangles or circles, as it is generally used for three-dimensional pieces of work, such as boxes. Plastic canvas is also available in sheets, which can be cut into different shapes without fraying.

Other evenweave fabrics, such as strong linen, can be used, but canvas will provide a stronger background for pieces which need to be hardwearing.

Threads

Generally the type of thread used for needlepoint must be related to the finished article. Always buy all the yarn before you begin a project, as dye lots can change and even a slight variation will show, especially across a large area of one colour.

When you have chosen your thread, work a test piece on the chosen canvas to gauge how the finished piece will look. For covering the canvas and providing an even, hardwearing fabric you need to use wool. Tapestry, crewel and Persian yarns are the usual wool threads for canvaswork. Nowadays advanced stitchers also use a range of different threads for experimental work in which sections of canvas may be left unworked or only partially covered, but it is advisable to use the traditional yarns when you begin, so that you get the feel of the stitches and the canvas before embarking on different pieces of work.

Estimating the quantity

Taking note of how much yarn you are cutting, work a 1in (2.5cm) square on the chosen canvas and using the chosen yarn and stitch. To estimate how much yarn will be needed for the design, multiply the amount of yarn used for the test by the number of square inches (2.5cm squares) of canvas to be stitched.

Wools

Tapestry wool is made especially for needlepoint. It is a fairly thick, firm, well-twisted yarn used as a single strand and is available in a good range or colours. Tapestry wool can be bought in skeins or as hanks (grounding wool).

Crewel wool is a fine, 2-ply yarn, which can be used singly or in groups. This makes it perfect for blending different colours together in the needle to create muted, tweedy shades.

Persian wool is slightly thicker than crewel wool. This yarn is made up of three loosely-twisted strands which can be separated either for working with one or two strands on fine canvas or for blending different colours together.

Two strands of Persian wool is equivalent to three lengths of crewel wool and one length of tapestry wool.

Rug yarn is a thick wool available in various weights from 2 to 8 ply, to be used in conjunction with rug canvas.

Other yarns

Stranded cotton is a loosely-twisted, lustrous thread that can be easily split up into six strands. It can be used as a single strand or in groups.

Nine strands of stranded cotton is equal to a single length of tapestry wool.

Soft embroidery cotton is a fairly thick, matt single yarn.

Silk yarns can also be used for canvaswork, but they are expensive, so use sparingly.

Metallic threads can be mixed in or used over previously stitched sections.

Knitting yarns can also be used but choose strong smooth yarns to obtain an evenly stitched result.

Ribbons and braids - $1/16$in (1.5mm) wide - can be used for small areas of decorative stitching.

Once you have become used to canvaswork stitching, you can experiment with different types of yarns and threads.

Needles

Tapestry needles are used for canvas embroidery
because they have rounded points which do not
split the yarn or the canvas threads. These needles
also have large eyes to accommodate the different
threads and yarns, which makes threading easier.
They range in size from 13 to 26. Remember the
higher the number, the finer the needle.

When gauging the correct needle for the canvas and
yarn, check that the needle eye is large enough to
enable the yarn to be threaded without fraying and
that the threaded needle can pass through the canvas
without forcing the threads apart.

Use a size 18 or 20 for general work with 13 for
coarse work and 24 or 26 for fine canvases.

Frames

Only plastic canvas can be worked in the hand
without a frame. All other canvases, unless very
small, must be set in a frame to hold them taut and
in shape while being stitched and when stored.

When canvas is set in a frame the stitches will be
properly formed in two movements - through the
canvas, then back to the right side again. One hand
should remain on the surface and the other on the
underside. The resulting movements will maintain
an even tension and help to keep the canvas from
distorting. Mount the canvaswork in either a
square or a rectangular frame. Never use a round
embroidery hoop, which will distort the canvas
threads when the two halves are pressed together.

Frames, right to left: rotating, stretcher and floor-standing

Simple stretcher frames can be quickly constructed at home either from two pairs of artists' stretchers - these lengths of wood have mitred and slotted corners which are then quickly fixed together - or from four pieces of wood which are mitred and fixed together with glue and nails in the same way as a picture frame.

Rotating frames, available commercially, have two side slats combined with two horizontal rollers to each of which a strip of webbing is attached. The frame is slotted together with screws or pegs, which are then used to tighten and hold the canvas taut. Floor-standing, rotating frames are also available which are lightweight enough to be moved around.

Thread organizer

When working with a variety of different coloured threads, it is a good idea to store them on an organizer. These are easy to make from stiff card.

Cut a strip of card and punch holes vertically down one long side. Thread each differently coloured yarn through one of the holes. Write the number of the shade alongside the hole. In this way the threads will not get muddled up in the workbox. This is also a useful way of keeping a record of the shades used in a particular project.

Ancillary equipment

Scissors - two pairs: a large, firm pair for cutting canvas and a small, sharp-pointed pair for trimming and cutting yarn.

Thimble - a useful piece of equipment when working a lot of embroidery as it will protect the middle (pushing) finger.

Masking tape - fold the tape over the rough canvas edges to protect the yarns and your hands when stitching (see page 19).

Strong buttonhole thread or fine string for attaching the canvas to a rotating frame or **drawing pins (thumb tacks)** for holding the canvas on a simple stretcher frame (see page 20).

A daylight bulb will help you to distinguish different colours at night or on gloomy days.

For designing and transferring designs you will need **tracing and graph papers.** A thick black water-proof **felt tip pen, crayons, ruler** and **set square**.

For blocking the finished piece of canvaswork you will need a **firm board** and large sheet of **blotting paper, sponge** and **rustless drawing pins (thumb tacks).**

Part 2:
TECHNIQUES

FITTING CANVAS INTO A FRAME

If the piece of canvaswork is very small it can be
worked in the hand, however, it is advisable to
work in a tapestry frame, as this minimizes the
amount of distortion to the finished piece.

Rotating frame

A standard rotating frame (see page 16) comes in a
range of sizes. You will find it easier if the frame is
the correct size for the canvas width. This means
that the webbing tape should be the same width or
wider than the canvas and the side bars should be
the same length or shorter (a longer canvas can be
wound onto the rollers).

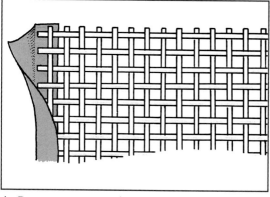

1 Cut your canvas to the correct size for the
design, i.e. at least 3in (7.5cm) larger than the
design all around. Cut and fold a length of masking
tape evenly in half over both raw side edges. Using
a contrasting thread, mark the centre of the canvas
both widthwise and lengthwise with a line of
tacking stitches.

2 Mark the centre of the webbing strip on each roller with a marking pen or pencil.

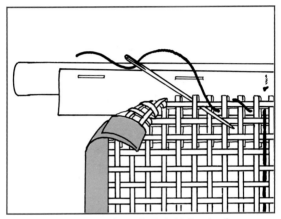

3 Turn over approximately ⅝in(1.5cm) of canvas at the top and, matching centre of canvas to centre mark on tape, oversew securely to attach the canvas to the webbing tape of the top roller. Begin stitching in the centre and work out towards the edge on both sides. Repeat, to oversew the base of the canvas to the webbing strip on the opposite roller in the same way.

4 Wind any surplus canvas around the rollers and tighten the screws at each side to hold it firmly in place.

5 Using buttonhole thread or fine string, lace the side edges of the canvas around the side laths of the frame (see page 21). If the canvas has been wound around the rollers, this lacing will have to be redone each time a new section of the canvas is unwound ready to be worked.

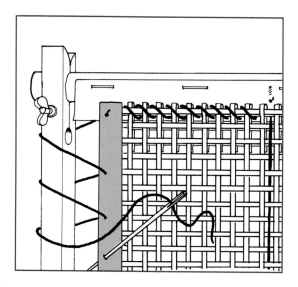

Simple stretcher frame

The working canvas needs to be the same size as this type of frame.

1 Prepare the canvas by sticking masking tape over all four edges. Alternatively, turn under approximately $5/8$in(1.5cm) on all four edges.

2 Place the canvas over the frame and fix a drawing pin in the centre top edge. Pull the canvas taut and fix a drawing pin in the centre bottom edge. Repeat for each side.

3 Fix drawing pins next in each corner, always making sure that the canvas is taut, then use more drawing pins along all the sides to attach the canvas securely and evenly.

WORKING FROM A CHART

Each square on a chart usually represents one stitch. The yarn colour will be denoted either by a similar printed colour or by a symbol.

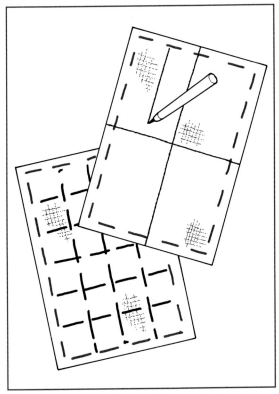

1 Measuring from the central lines of tacking stitches, mark the outer edges of the design using a contrasting tacking stitch. Subdivide the canvas again into an even number of threads, such as ten, and work tacking stitches or mark with a pen across the canvas. Then mark across the chart in the same way. Ten is a convenient number as charts often have thicker lines marking every ten squares. Some canvas is already marked in this way.

2 When following a chart, each symbol represents the colour and stitch that should be worked in that position on the canvas. Match the symbol to the yarn colour and work the number of stitches shown by the number of squares containing this same symbol on the chart. Use the tacked lines as a guide to count the squares on the canvas which correspond to the squares of the chart.

Starting point

The point at which you start stitching a design is a matter of preferenc: you can either begin with the largest motif or start from the top line.

To work a chart line by line, you will need several needles. Thread each colour needed in the first row of the chart into a separate needle and work the row. Once each colour is finished, bring the needle to the front of the work to avoid a tangle of threads behind.

DESIGNING

Needlepoint charts

Designing your own chart for working in tent or cross stitch, will produce a unique piece of embroidery. You will need tracing and graph paper. Also available is traced grid paper, which is tracing paper ready printed with a grid.

Choose a motif or design with a clear outline but
remember that as you draw up the design you can
always leave out various sections or simplify any
complicated edges.

A well-spaced background is essential to a good
design. You may need to redraw the design several
times until the result looks ready for stitching. If
you are worried about your ability to draw objects
or motifs, trace off a design from a book, a
magazine or from one of the printed labels from
bottles or packages around the house.

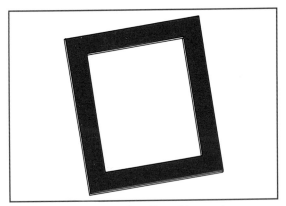

Make a window out of cardboard by cutting a
square of card; mark and cut out the centre. Use
this when searching for suitable motifs as it will help
to isolate the motifs and give you an impression of
what a chosen shape will look like by itself.

1 Pick out your motif or design and tape it flat on a
surface. Cut a piece of tracing or traced graph paper
and tape it flat over the design. Using a sharp pencil
or fine-tipped marking pen, draw around the

outline of the design. (Follow the outline of the squares if using traced graph paper.) Alter the outline as necessary to gain a more even motif. Add in the details within the outline.

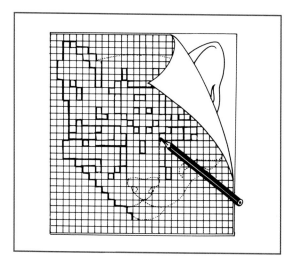

2 Cut a piece of graph paper to the same size as the tracing paper. Transfer the outline from the tracing paper to the graph paper. Match the grids together if using traced graph paper.

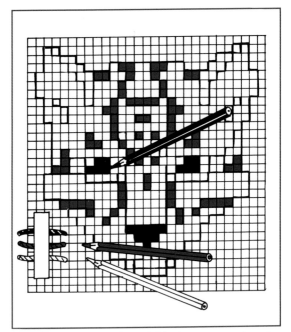

3 Use crayons or coloured felt tip pens to colour in the outline. Either follow the original colours of the motif or change the shades to suit your own ideas. To try out different colourways, photostat the design and colour it in different colours until you have the result you want. To help match the crayon colours to thread colours, make a key at the side of the drawing: colour in a square of graph paper and tape a short length of the thread you have selected beside it.

Working with a tracing

Designs can also be drawn directly onto the canvas as an outline or coloured with pens to make them easier to follow. A quick method to enlarge a design to the correct size is to use a photocopier.

1 Draw up the full size design on a sheet of paper and mark over the outline with a thick black felt tip pen to gain a firm outline.

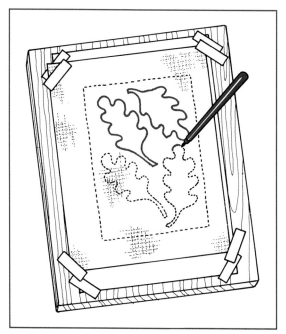

2 Tape the design flat on a board. Tape the canvas centrally over the top. The design should show through between the canvas threads. Now simply go over the design lines again with a water soluble pen to mark the canvas.

ADAPTING PATTERNS

If the pattern you wish to use is the wrong size for the situation in which the needlepoint will be displayed, it is possible to make modifications.

Changing size

To enlarge or reduce a design, change the canvas size but remember also that this will affect the needle size as well as the thickness and possibly the amount of wool needed. Count up the horizontal and the vertical squares on the charted design and divide by the mesh count of the canvas to find the finished size. For example, a chart covering 140 by 130 squares will produce a piece measuring 14 x 13in (36 x 33cm) on a 10hpi canvas or 8 ³/₄ x 8 ¹/₄in (22.5 x 21cm) on a 16hpi canvas.

The table on pages 92 to 93 gives a range of popular chart and canvas sizes as a ready reckoner.

A design can also be enlarged by adding a "frame": either one or two plain-coloured borders in shades picked out from the main image or a border with a simple geometric pattern, such as those shown on pages 29 to 31. To add a more complex border, follow the instructions below.

Creating a neat corner design

Use a mirror to create a good corner when designing a border or pattern.

1 Place a small mirror diagonally across the design. Check the reflected image and move the mirror

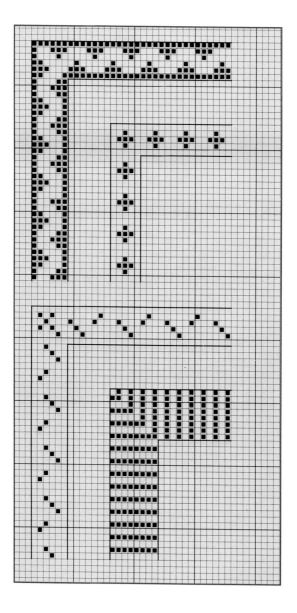

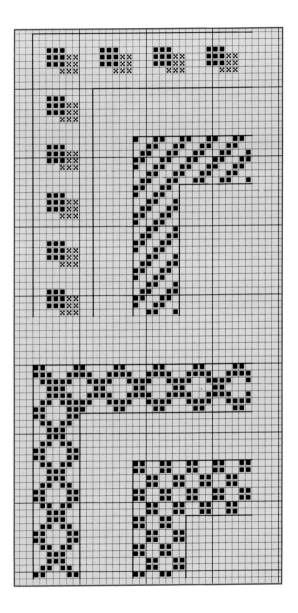

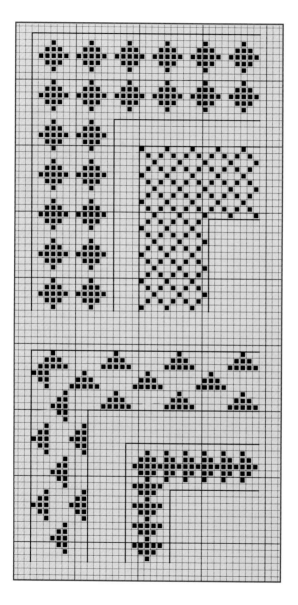

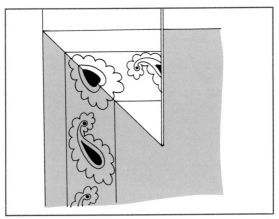

slowly down the border until the design looks good in the mirror.

2 Mark a line diagonally across the design, then remove the mirror.

3 Cut and tape a piece of tracing paper over the design and trace off the design up to the diagonal line. Turn the tracing paper over and mark the

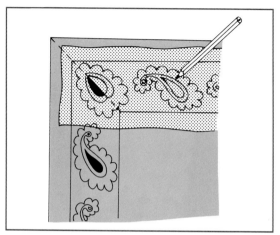

design in reverse from the other side of diagonal line. Repeat at each corner of the design.

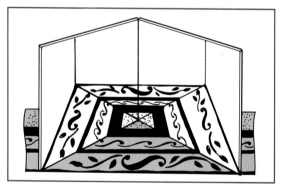

This method can also be used to create a square design from a border design. Lay the border design horizontally on a flat surface. Place two mirrors at right angles to each other. Move the mirrors backwards and forwards until an attractive design is achieved, then mark both ends with diagonal lines and trace as before.

STARTING OFF

Threading a needle

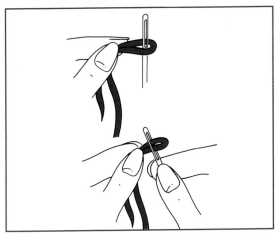

To thread the needle, wrap the thread(s) over the needle eye and hold tight. Slip the thread loop off the needle and push the loop through the eye.

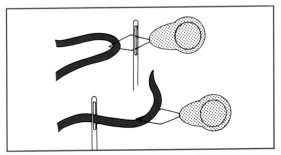

If you have a problem threading needles use a needle threader. Push the needle threader through the eye of the needle. Loop the thread through the threader and pull it back though the needle eye.

Beginning the first length of yarn

1 Thread the needle and knot the free end of yarn. Insert the needle from the front of the canvas to the back, ¾in (2cm) in front of where the stitching will begin, leaving the knot on the right side.

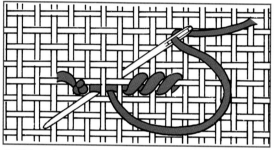

2 Bring the needle to the front and work a few stitches over the canvas and yarn end. When you reach the knot, cut it off and continue stitching.

3 Subsequent lengths of yarn can be starting by sliding the needle under the backs of a few stitches, before taking the needle to the right side .

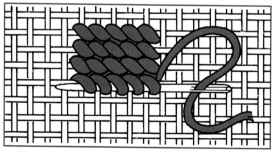

4 To end a length of yarn, take the needle to the back of the work, then slide it under a few stitches. Trim off the end.

Tension

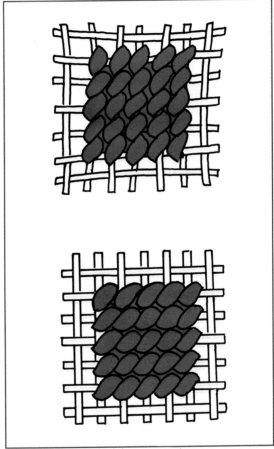

Above: tension too tight; below: even tension

Try to keep an even tension when stitching. If you are in any doubt, practise on a spare piece of canvas before you begin. Keep checking on the tension.

If it is too loose, the stitches will not cover the canvas properly, if too tight, the canvas will pucker and stretch out of shape.

When stitching, try to bring the needle up out of the canvas through an empty hole and go into the canvas through a partially filled hole. In this way the yarns are smoothed down throughout the whole work.

JOINING CANVAS

When working a large project two or more pieces of canvas may need to be joined together to create a piece of canvas of the right dimensions. Seaming canvas together can be done in three ways.

With edges butted together

This method is suitable for plastic canvas. Simply trim off the canvas to exactly the right size. Place the two pieces with edges butting together and the grid matching across the join. Whip stitch the two edges together, then work a needlepoint stitch over the stitches to hide the join.

With folded edges

A method for joining pieces of worked canvas together. The separate canvases should be blocked first (see page 40).

1 Trim away the excess canvas from both sides, leaving a margin of $5/8$in (1.5cm) or 2in (5cm) on larger items.

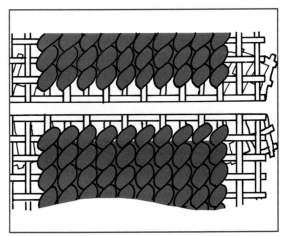

2 Fold under the spare canvas leaving one horizontal or one vertical unworked thread (depending where the join is) on each edge.

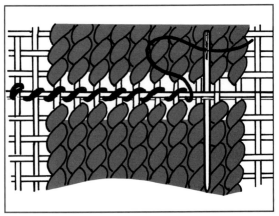

3 Working from the right side and matching the canvas grid exactly across the join, use a strong buttonhole thread to whip the folded edges securely together.

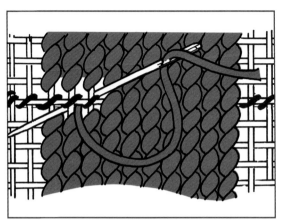

4 Complete the needlepoint stitches across the join.

With overlapped edges

This method is used to join pieces of unworked canvas together.

1 Leave a border of ½ to ¾in (1 to 2cm) of unworked canvas along the edges to be joined.

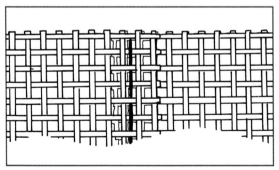

2 Working right side up, overlap the two edges matching the canvas grid exactly and tack together.

3 Work the stitches of the design through both pieces of canvas.

BLOCKING THE FINISHED WORK

When a piece of needlepoint is complete you might find that it has been pulled out of shape, so that the corners no longer form right angles. To correct this, the canvas will need to be blocked, that is, stretched back into shape. If there is only a slight distortion, just give the canvas a good press with a steam iron over a damp cloth, pulling it carefully into shape by hand. If the distortion is marked, work as follows:

1 Dampen the wrong side of the worked canvas using a wet cloth or water spray. Do not overwet the canvas, the water is just used to soften the canvas, so that it can be pulled back into shape. Check first that the yarns do not run. If they do, try to correct the distortion using a steam iron as described above.

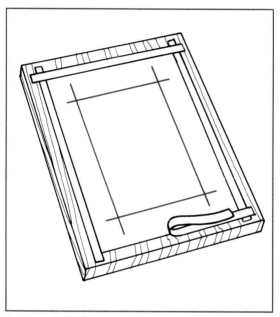

2 On a clean sheet of paper mark out the finished outline of the design with accurate right angles and using a waterproof pen. Tape this paper onto a piece of board.

3 Lay the canvas right side down over the board and, using rustless drawing pins (thumb tacks), fix in place through the canvas around the worked section, matching the outline of the needlepoint to the marked outline on the board. Begin with a tack in each corner, then tack the centre points on each

side, then add drawing pins (thumb tacks) evenly spaced – approximately 1in (2.5cm) apart - in between. Check that the canvas is straight and leave to dry out for at least 24 hours.

Remove the canvas and check the corners for right angles. If there is still a marked distorion, repeat the blocking process.

Mounting Canvas for a Picture

A picture frame will have a backing board to which the canvas should be laced, so that it is kept flat. It is a matter of personal preference as to whether or not glass is used in the frame. Glass will protect the embroidery but will tend to dull the colour of the yarns and flatten the texture. If you choose not to have glass, you can use a protective spray over the needlepoint which will help to keep it clean.

Make sure that the rebate of the picture frame is deep enough to take the thickness of the embroidery and canvas wrapped around the backing board.

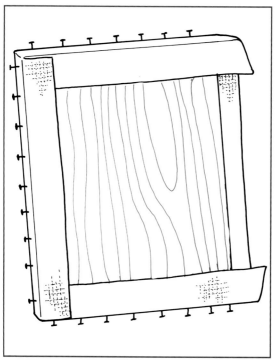

1 Place the finished piece right side up over the backing board and pin the top edge into the edge of the board. Pull the canvas over the base edge and

pin into the bottom edge of the board. Repeat to
stretch the canvas over each side. Check that the
design is centred over the board and adjust if
necessary.

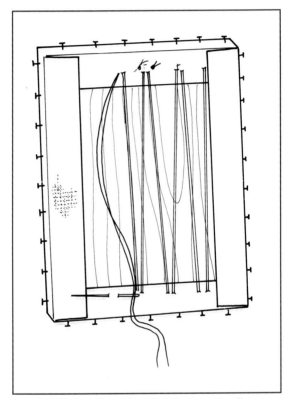

2 Thread a needle with a doubled length of
buttonhole twist and, beginning in the centre of
one side, lace the unworked canvas across the board
to the corner. Pull the threads taut. Go back to the
centre and lace out to the opposite corner in the
same way.

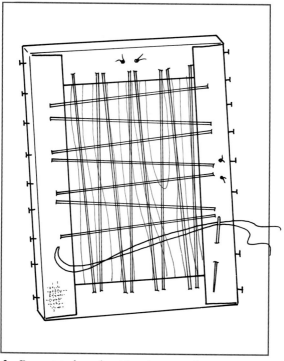

3 Repeat to lace the side edges together.

4 Place the mounted board into the frame, add glass (if desired) and secure at the back with small pins or clips.

NEEDLEPOINT CUSHIONS

Needlepoint embroidery makes a very attractive cushion front. Once the stitching is finished, trim the edges of the canvas leaving a ⅝in (1.5cm) unworked border all around. Three methods for making up the cushion are described below.

Making cushion with plain back

1 Cut a piece of backing fabric to the same size as the trimmed canvas. Place backing and canvas with right sides together. Pin and machine stitch around the cushion following the outside edges of the needlepoint and leaving an opening centrally in one side, the base edge.

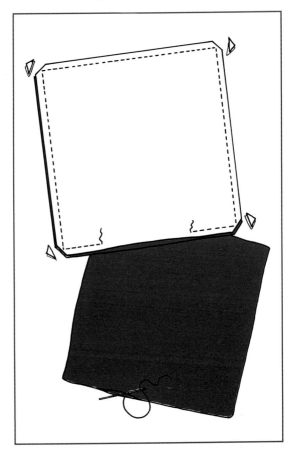

2 Trim off the corners and along the edges, then turn the cushion cover right side out. Insert the cushion pad. Turn in the edges of the opening in line with the remainder of the seam and slipstitch together.

Making cushion with centre back zipper

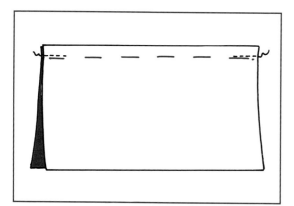

1 Use a zipper 2in (5cm) shorter than the width of the cushion front. For the back cut a piece of fabric to the same width and 1 ¼in (3cm) longer than the canvas. Fold in half top to bottom and cut along the fold to form two sections. Place the back pieces with right sides together; pin and tack together giving a ⅝in(1.5cm) seam. Machine stitch in from each side for 1in (2.5cm). Press the seam open.

2 Place the zipper right side down over the wrong side of the tacked section of the seam; pin and tack the zipper in place. Turn the fabric over and, working from the right side, stitch in place all

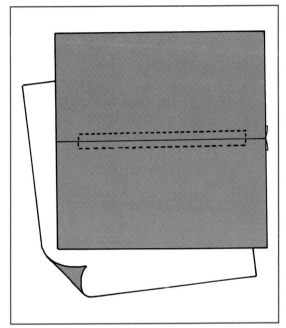

around zipper. Remove the tacking threads.

3 Complete the cover by stitching the front to the back in the same way as described above.

Making cushion with a frame of fabric

1 Decide on the border width and cut four pieces of fabric as follows:

– two strips to the chosen border width and to the length of the sides of the worked area of the canvas plus twice the border width plus twice the seam allowance;

– two strips to the chosen border width and to the

length of the top and bottom of the worked area of the canvas plus twice the border width plus twice the seam allowance.

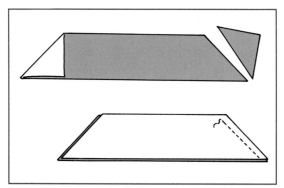

2 Take each strip and fold each end diagonally in line with the opposite; press. Unfold and cut along the diagonal line.

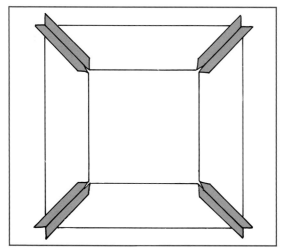

3 Place the pieces together in order; pin and stitch

the diagonal seams to within ⅝in (1.5cm) of the
inner edge to form a frame. Press the seams open.

4 Place the wrong side of the fabric frame centrally
on top of the right side of the worked canvas.
Tuck under the seam allowances on all four sides of
the fabric frame and pin in place to the needlepoint.
The seams at the mitred corners should open out to
give neat right angles.

5 Using a thread to match the fabric frame, slipstitch around the inner edges of the frame with
small stitches to attach it to the needlepoint.

6 Cut a piece of backing to match the framed size
of the cushion front. Place the cushion front to the
backing right sides together and complete the cover
in the same way as described above.

HANGING NEEDLEPOINT

As an alternative to framing, but perhaps not so permanent, a piece of needlepoint can be hung from a dowel rod. The needlepoint is backed with a piece of cotton or closely-woven linen lining in a harmonizing colour. It can then be fixed to a dowel rod, painted or varnished to suit the work.

1 Cut the canvas edges to within 1in (2.5cm) of the worked section. Cut a piece of lining fabric to the same size. Turn in the edges of the canvas along the edge of the finished stitches, so that no unworked canvas shows on the right side.

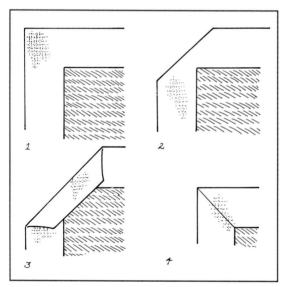

2 Mitre the corners, by trimming the canvas diagonally across the corners ½in (1cm) from the stitches, then folding in the corner diagonally before folding down the sides. Slipstitch in position.

3 Turn in the raw edges of the lining, mitring the corners in the same way.

4 Place the lining over the needlepoint, wrong sides together and matching the outer edges; pin and tack together. Measure down from the top edge for ½in (1cm) and mark on either side, then measure around the dowel rod and mark this measurement below the first mark. This will be the size of the gap for the rod.

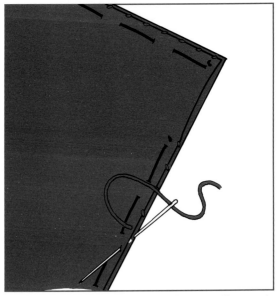

5 Slipstitch the lining to the needlepoint all around, leaving openings between the marks.

6 Insert the rod, add brass or wood knobs at either end and fix a piece of hanging cord between the knobs and the rod. Hang from a picture hook.

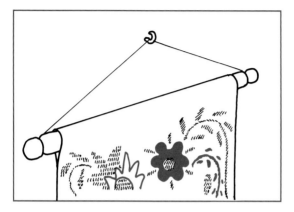

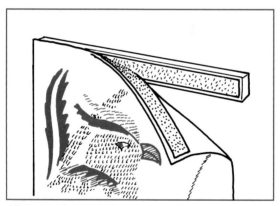

Alternatively, stitch down the lining completely, then stitch a strip of touch and close fastening along the top edge on the lining side of the hanging and attach this to the opposite half of the fastening tape which has been stuck to a length of battening fixed to the wall.

The same could be done at the bottom of the piece to make the hanging rigid.

CORRECTING MISTAKES

Reworking stitches

If you have made a mistake when stitching a piece of canvaswork, do not hesitate to unpick the error and rework the canvas.

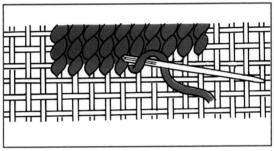

1 When unpicking only two or three stitches, unthread the needle and use the end to carefully ease out the yarn.

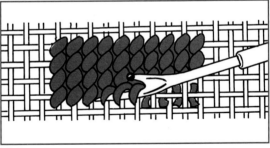

2 On a large area, use a pair of sharp-pointed scissors or a seam ripper to carefully cut through the stitches, then gently pull out the discarded yarn.

3 Do not reuse yarn that has been pulled out of the canvas, as it will have kinked and worn and will spoil the look of the finished piece.

Repairing canvas

Sometimes when unpicking stitches, accidents can happen and the canvas threads are snipped by mistake. To repair a piece of canvas, a small new piece of canvas is overlaid to cover the hole.

1 Unpick the stitches around the hole to create an area about 1 1/2in (4cm) square.

2 Cut a piece of canvas the same gauge as the canvas you are repairing 1 1/2in (4cm) square.

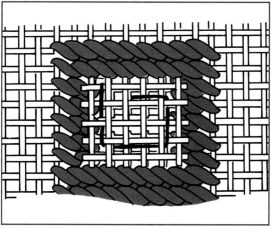

3 Position the patch on the wrong side of the canvas centrally over the hole. Line up the threads of the canvas with the patch and tack in place.

4 Continue to embroider the canvas in the usual way but working over the two layers of canvas. The

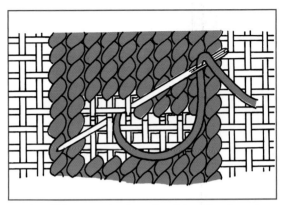

patch will be unnoticed on the right side when the
piece is completed.

COMBINING DIFFERENT GRADES OF CANVAS

Combining two or more different gauge canvases
will allow you to work small pieces of detailed
design within areas of larger stitching.

This is particularly appropriate for landscape
pictures: the foreground can be worked in a coarse
gauge canvas, the middle ground in a medium grade
canvas and the distance in a fine canvas. The
technique could also be used to stitch a central
scene, perhaps showing figures, surrounded by an
abstract patterned border Fine canvas would be
used to give a more realistic representation of the
people.

There are two methods of adding a different grade
canvas to the original piece – overlapping and
grafting – as described below.

Overlapping

Two pieces can be overlapped but this can be bulky and not so strong. To do this, herringbone stitch around the edges. Add a dab of fabric adhesive to keep the edges from fraying.

Grafting

Another way is to graft two pieces of canvas together. This results in a double thickness of canvas which makes a hardwearing piece.

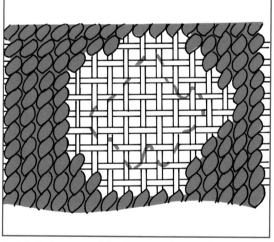

1 Mark the area of the finer grade motif on the larger hole canvas, then embroider the design on the larger hole canvas to within one or two holes all around.

2 Cut a piece of finer gauge canvas to the size of the motif plus a border of 2in (5cm) all around, then stitch the motif.

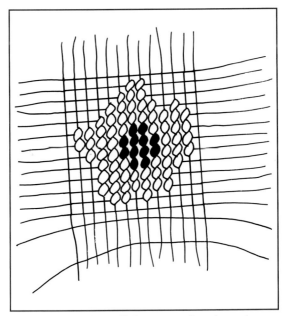

3 Gently withdraw all the canvas threads on the finer canvas, up to the outside stitches of the worked section, leaving the rest of the canvas threads loose.

4 Using a contrasting sewing thread, tack the finer piece centrally over the marked section on the larger hole canvas.

5 Thread the loose threads of the finer canvas through the larger hole canvas to the wrong side, then weave them into the back of the stitching.

6 Complete the stitching of the design on the larger hole canvas around and up to the finer canvas piece (see page 59). Trim away the tacking stitches.

COLOUR CHANGES

Some designs, particularly free-style pieces, look
good if only part of the area has been stitched,
leaving the rest of the canvas blank. By spraying or
painting the canvas first, the effect can look slightly
three dimensional.

Painting

Either use fabric paints or spray paints which will
not run and ruin the yarn when the piece is being
blocked. If you are unsure of the result, practise on
a spare piece of canvas first.

Stencilling

White canvas can be stencilled to enhance a design.
Stencils are also ideal for marking shapes to be
stitched onto canvas. A stencil can be held firm or
turned about the canvas to create layers of different
shapes or a blur of different colours.

1 Draw up the stencil onto a piece of thin card and cut out.

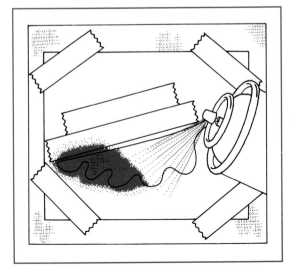

2 Use masking tape to hold the stencil firmly on the canvas and to mask off any areas that you wish to mark in a different colour. Spray paint, then leave to dry completely.

3 When dry, remove the stencil and reposition. Unmask previous sections of the stencil and mask those already painted. Spray again. Leave to dry.

4 Remove the stencil and embroider sections of the design to bring them out in relief against the flat background.

Space dyeing the yarns

Space dyeing is an inexpensive way of creating subtle, variegated yarn shades. Use cold water dyes and mix and match colours to produce a range of different effects.

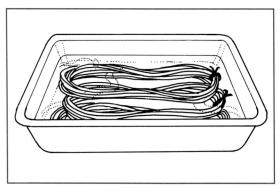

1 Wind each length of yarn into a long hank and tie loosely. Soak the yarn hanks in water for several hours. Squeeze out excess water and leave in a shallow dish.

2 Make up a salt solution with 2oz (50g) of salt to ½pt (500ml) of hot water. Mix each dye up separately in a jar. Mix half a teaspoon of dye with a tablespoon of salt solution; stir until dissolved. Add more hot water until the jar is half full.

3 Spoon the dyes over the threads at intervals allowing the colours to overlap and merge together. Leave in the dyes for five to ten minutes, then check for colour absorption.

4 If satisfied with the result, dilute 4oz (100g) of washing soda in ³⁄₄pt (450ml) of hot water. Pour this solution over the dyed threads and leave for approximately 30 minutes to set the dyes.

5 Pour away the liquid; rinse out the yarns thoroughly. Wash in detergent; rinse in warm water and leave to dry. Keep the dyed yarns wound around a cardboard inner tube roll.

Part 3:
STITCHES

Needlepoint designs are most commonly worked in tent stitch - small diagonally worked stitches. Tent stitches on a narrow mesh canvas can interpret fine design lines and introduce some shading to reproduce realistic natural designs, such as birds, animals, fruits and flowers.

Ornamental stitches interpret a design through shape and texture. The reproduction of natural motifs will be less detailed since ornamental stitches are generally larger than tent stitches.

Florentine stitches, which are straight stitches of varying lengths worked parallel to the vertical canvas threads, are stitched in zigzag lines to produce the wavy abstract patterns characteristic of Florentine or bargello work.

Note: For reasons of space in the diagrams, the needles are shown going into and out of the canvas in one movement. However, as mentioned above, each stitch should be made in two movements (see page 14).

TENT (CONTINENTAL) STITCH
Small diagonal stitches worked horizontally across the canvas. This stitch looks like half cross stitch (see below) from the front, but on the wrong side the stitches appear as longer diagonal stitches. This stitch is hardwearing but can distort the canvas. It uses more yarn than half cross stitch.

The rows are worked from left to right. It is preferable to work all the rows in the same

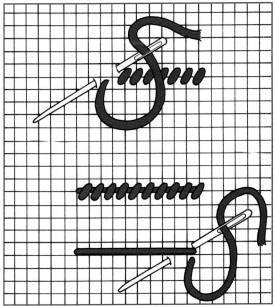

Top: Tent (continental) stitch; centre and below: tramming tent stitch

direction, otherwise a ridged effect is produced.

Tent stitch can also be trammed to give a more hardwearing finish. In this case, work a trammed stitch from left to right, then bring the needle through vertically one thread down. Insert again one thread vertically above and make the stitches in the normal way.

TENT (BASKETWEAVE) STITCH

This method of working tent stitch is suitable for large areas and causes less distortion The name refers to the effect produced on the wrong side.

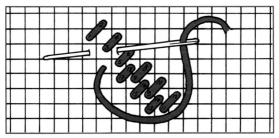

The stitch is worked diagonally across the canvas and is produced by taking the needle diagonally over one intersection then vertically underneath two horizontal threads for rows going from top to bottom, and over one intersection and horizontally underneath two vertical threads for rows going in the opposite direction.

HALF CROSS STITCH

Use this stitch instead of tent stitch when working with a thicker yarn. Half cross stitch resembles tent stitch but the working method is different. Half cross stitch consists of small diagonal stitches worked over one canvas thread intersection.

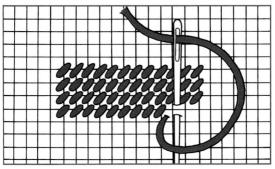

On the reverse side the stitches are vertical. It is

not as hardwearing as tent stitch but produces less
distortion of the canvas.

CROSS STITCH

Bring the needle up through the canvas and insert at
A, two threads up and two threads to the left. Bring
the needle out at B, two threads vertically down,
forming half the cross. To complete the cross, insert
the needle at C, two threads up and two threads to
the right.

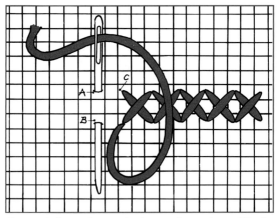

Cross stitch can be worked several at a time. Work
a row of the first half of the stitch from right to left,
then go back from left to right completing the
crosses. Alternatively, work each complete cross
before starting the next, but make sure that all the
upper diagonal stitches face in the same direction.

DOUBLE CROSS STITCH

When completed, this stitch forms a square over

four horizontal and four vertical canvas threads.

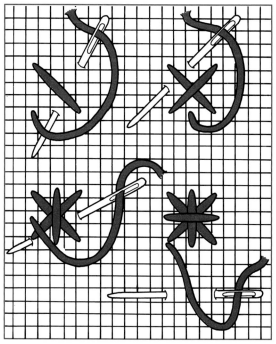

Work a standard cross stitch, then bring the needle out in the centre of the base of the cross. Take a stitch vertically to the centre of the top of the cross, bringing the needle out centrally on the left of the cross. Take a horizontal stitch over the cross, bringing the needle out at the base of the cross ready for the next stitch.

SPLIT TRAMMED STITCH
On double thread canvas the needle is brought up in between the two intersecting canvas threads.

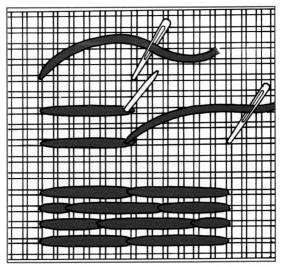

Carry the yarn the required distance, no longer than 13cm (5in), and insert through the canvas again between two vertical double threads. Bring the needle back up just to the left of the same thread and through the centre of the yarn. Continue in this way to the end of the row.

Place the stitches in the next and all subsequent rows so that they do not begin or end at the same pair of vertical threads.

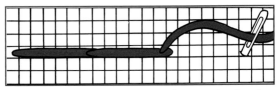

On single canvas, work in a similar way, but leaving two horizontal canvas threads between each row of tramming.

UPRIGHT GOBELIN STITCH

Work vertical straight stitches close together over
two threads of canvas. The second and subsequent
rows are stitched immediately underneath, working
in the opposite direction.

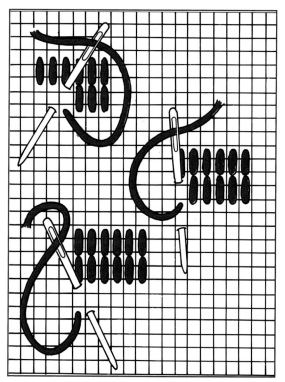

This stitch can be worked over trammed stitches
(see above) to give a raised effect. Work a trammed
stitch from left to right, then bring the needle
through one thread down and one thread to the
left. Insert again two threads above. and bring out
two threads down and one thread to the left.

ENCROACHING GOBELIN STITCH

Ideal for shading, this variation of upright gobelin stitch produces a closely worked fabric effect. The diagonal stitches are worked in rows from right to left and left to right.

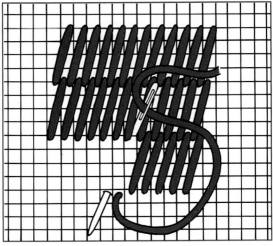

Work each stitch over five horizontal canvas threads and diagonally across one vertical canvas thread.

Work the following rows in the same way.
Stitches in the second and subsequent rows should overlap the previous row by one horizontal canvas thread.

GOBELIN FILLING STITCH

Rows of vertical straight stitches are worked alternately from left to right and right to left, with second and subsequent rows overlapping.

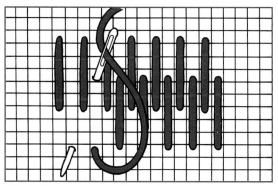

Work the first row, taking each stitch over six horizontal canvas threads and leaving two vertical canvas threads between each stitch. Work the second row from right to left and fit the stitches evenly between the stitches of the first row. Any gaps in the first and last row are filled with straight stitches worked over three canvas threads.

BRICK STITCH

This is very similar to Gobelin filling stitch but the stitches are shorter.

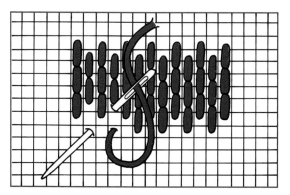

Work the first row taking each stitch over two horizontal threads and leaving two vertical threads between each one. Work the following rows in between, beginning the stitches halfway up those in the previous row (see page 73).

PLAIT STITCH

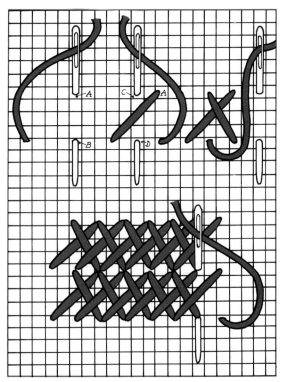

Work this stitch in horizontal rows from left to right. Bring the needle out of the canvas and insert at A, four canvas threads up and four canvas threads to the right. Bring the needle out again at B, four canvas threads down. Insert the needle at C four threads up and two threads to the left and bring out, four canvas threads down at D. Continue in this way. Each row is worked directly under the one above.

RICE STITCH (WILLIAM AND MARY STITCH)
A cross stitch with a diamond worked over the top. Use a thicker thread for the cross stitches and a finer thread for the diagonal back stitches.

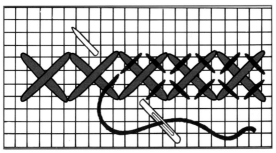

Cover the working area with cross stitches worked over two or four canvas threads. Use the finer yarn to work small diagonal back stitches at right angles over one or two canvas threads, so that the stitches also form mini crosses.

KELIM STITCH
This diagonal stitch, formed by two rows, looks like a knitted stocking stitch.

Work in either vertical or horizontal rows, taking a

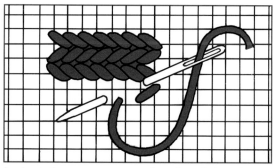

back stitch over two canvas threads and changing the diagonal direction with each row.

Hungarian Stitch

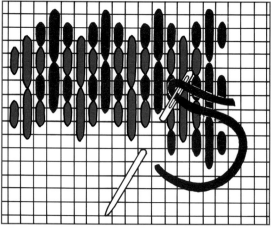

A stitch formed by working a group of stitches. Each group consists of three vertical stitches worked over two, four and two horizontal canvas threads, with two vertical threads left between each group of stitches. Each subsequent row fits into the preceding row. The groups can be worked in two different coloured yarns.

SCOTTISH STITCH

This is also a group stitch, which should be worked in one or two coloured yarns for maximum effect.

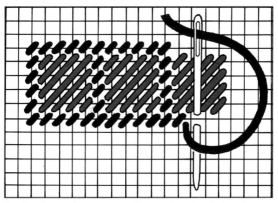

In the first colour, work diagonal satin stitches in squares over one, two, three, four, three, two and one intersections of canvas threads. Leave one vertical thread between each square in a row and one horizontal thread between the rows.

Once the squares are complete, change to the second colour and outline the squares in half cross stitch worked over one intersection of canvas.

CHEQUER STITCH

This group stitch is made up of alternate squares of diagonal satin stitch and tent stitch. Chequer stitch can be worked in one or two colours.

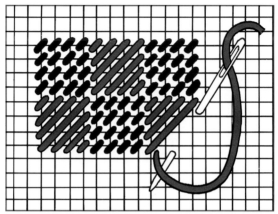

Each of the squares that make up this stitch is
worked over four horizontal and four vertical
threads of canvas. Work the squares in diagonal
rows beginning at the upper lefthand corner.

DIAGONAL STITCH

This is worked in groups of four stitches diagonally
across the canvas.

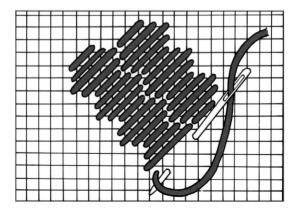

Bring the needle through the canvas and work
diagonal straight stitches over two, three, four and
three canvas intersections. Work the second row,
placing the longest stitch of the second row diagonally below the shortest stitch of the row above.

MOSAIC (CUSHION) STITCH

Each adjacent square of this group stitch is worked
in a different direction. Use one or two different
coloured yarns for full effect.

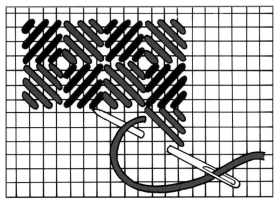

Work a group of five diagonal stitches to form a
square by working over one, two, three, two and
one canvas thread intersections. Work the square
alongside in the opposite direction.

MILANESE STITCH

Worked in four diagonal lines, this stitch forms a
pattern of triangles pointing alternately upwards and
downwards. It is made up of four back stitches
worked in different lengths in diagonal rows.

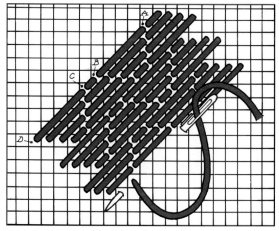

1 Bring the needle through the canvas at A and take a back stitch over one thread up and one thread to the right. Bring the needle out five threads down and five threads to the left at B.

2 Insert the needle again four threads up and four threads to the right (at A). Bring the needle out five threads down and five threads to the left at C.

3 Insert the needle again one thread up and one thread to the right (at B) and bring out five threads down and five threads to the left at D.

4 Continue in this way. On the remaining three rows of the pattern, work back stitches over two and three, three and two, four and one canvas thread intersections.

CASHMERE STITCH
This stitch consists of a group of three diagonal

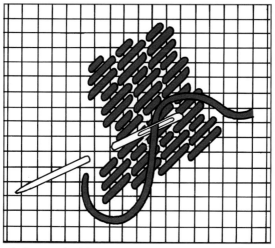

stitches worked in sequence over one, two and two canvas thread intersections. The end of each stitch in the group falls exactly beneath the others.

The group of three stitches moves one thread to the right each time when working diagonally downwards from left to right and one thread to the left when working upwards from right to left.

MOORISH STITCH

This stitch is made up of two different rows of diagonal stitches worked from the top lefthand to the lower righthand corner. It looks most effective when worked in two or more different colours.

Work the first row of diagonal stitches over two, three, four and three canvas thread intersections, with an extra stitch over two intersections to complete the square at the end of each row.

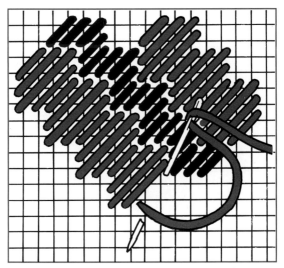

Work the second row in small diagonal stitches
worked over two canvas thread intersections
following the outline of the previous row to
produce a stepped effect. Repeat this sequence for
the next pair of rows.

JACQUARD STITCH

The stitches are arranged in rows to produce a
stepped effect. Work in one or two different
coloured threads to accentuate the pattern. The
rows of stitches are worked diagonally from the
upper lefthand side down to the lower righthand
side, and up again.

In the first row, the stitches are worked diagonally
over two canvas thread intersections.

In the second row, the stitches are worked

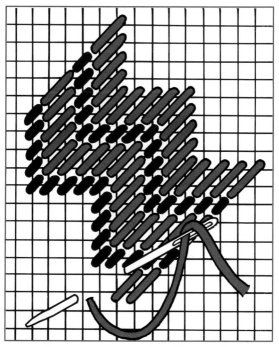

diagonally over one canvas thread intersection.
Repeat these two rows alternately.

BYZANTINE STITCH

Similar to Jacquard stitch but with stitches all of the
same length, these diagonally-worked stitches
produce a brocade effect.

Work satin stitches diagonally over four vertical and
four horizontal canvas threads (see page 84).

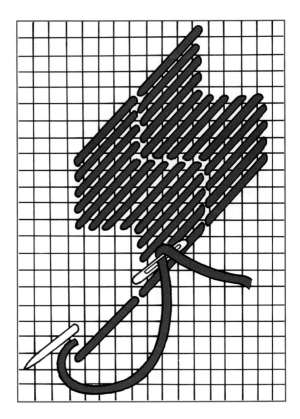

FLORENTINE (FLAME) STITCH

Used for working the zigzag patterns in Florentine or Bargello work, these are straight vertical stitches worked diagonally up and down the canvas forming "waves" of colour (see page 85). Generally used over large areas, the rows are worked in a variety of different colours. The size of the "wave" can vary, depending on the number and the length of the stitches worked.

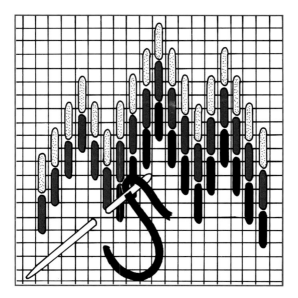

STAR STITCH

This stitch forms a star over six horizontal and six vertical canvas threads.

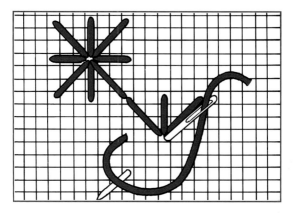

Work eight straight stitches over three canvas
threads from the outer edge of the square into the
same central hole. The stitch can be worked in
horizontal, vertical or diagonal rows.

RHODES STITCH

A raised filling stitch that covers a square of canvas
of an even number of canvas threads. In the
diagram below the stitch is being worked over six
horizontal and six vertical threads.

Begin with a diagonal stitch worked from the
bottom lefthand to the top righthand corner of the
square. Bring the needle out one thread to the
right and take it to one thread to the left. Continue
working anticlockwise around the square until all
the holes are filled, then finish off with a small vertical straight stitch at the centre worked through all
the layers of yarn and canvas to anchor the stitch.

VELVET (PLUSH) STITCH

An unusual needlepoint stitch as it results in a pile
fabric which can be trimmed to give 3D effects.

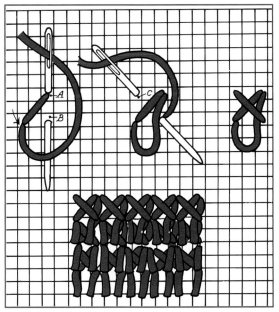

1 Work from left to right in horizontal rows from bottom upwards. Bring the needle out of the canvas and insert at A, two threads up and two threads to the right, coming out at the base of the diagonal stitch just formed.

2 Reinsert at A, leaving a loop of yarn and bring the needle out two threads down at B, keeping the thread above the needle.

3 Insert again two threads up and two threads to the left at C and bring out again at B ready for the next stitch.

4 When all the rows have been stitched, cut the loops of yarn and trim to the desired length.

Part 4:
CARE AND DISPLAY

CARING FOR NEEDLEPOINT

Store canvaswork rolled around a cardboard cylinder to prevent the formation of creases which will weaken the materials. If a piece must be folded, refold it at varying intervals folding the canvas across a different section. Store the rolled-up canvas in acid-free tissue paper in a dark, dry place.

Regularly vacuum canvaswork pieces to remove dust and grit which can rot the fibres. Large items can be hung outside on a washing line and beaten gently on the wrong side with a wooden spoon.

Canvaswork must always be dry cleaned professionally or at home with a upholstery foam cleaner. Water will remove the dressing and so soften the canvas, disturbing the smooth stitching.

When the finished canvaswork has been mounted on a chair it is best to dry clean it in situ rather than remove it. This will keep the canvas stretched into shape and prevent shrinkage. Small stains can be removed by dabbing with a small sponge soaked in white spirit.

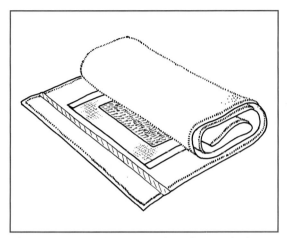

If you need to wash a piece of needlepoint before making up, test the yarns for colour fastness first by dabbing the yarn on the wrong side of the work with a piece of damp cotton wool, then gently washing in warm water with a mild soap. Rinse well, take out of the water and roll up in a towel to remove the excess moisture.

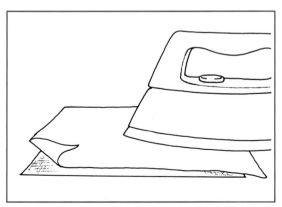

Lay the needlepoint flat to dry, until just damp,

then place on the ironing board, cover with a dry cloth and gently press or reblock back into shape.

DISPLAYING NEEDLEPOINT

Needlepoint can be displayed in a variety of different ways. Cushions are a particular favourite. To give the cushion an even edge all around, position any opening across a plain fabric back, then you can machine stitch all around the outer edge (see page 47). As well as the usual scatter cushions, try cushions with a small gusset making a box shape.

Stool tops and chair seats look very attractive worked in needlepoint and because the wool is strong, the resulting cover should last for many years. When stitching a stool top or chair seat make sure that you use one of the strong stitches, such as trammed tent stitch (see page 66), which covers the back of the canvas as well as the front.

Trays and firescreens have the added bonus of glass protection. The only drawback is that the glass can obscure the stitching and make the colours seem less vibrant.

Canvaswork can be a good fashion extra as well. Try stitching a smart belt or a bag front or even a hat band for a trilby. When the stitching is complete, give the finished result a spray with a water repellant spray to help protect against spills and as an added protection against dust and dirt.

READY RECKONER

A table to give a quick guide to the different dimensions produced by a range of canvas meshes. Figures are rounded up to the nearest 1/4in(0.5cm).

chart squares	10hpi	12hpi	14hpi
80	8in (20.5cm)	6 3/4in (17cm)	5 3/4in (15cm)
90	9in (23cm)	7 1/2in (19cm)	6 1/2in (16.5cm)
100	10in (25.5cm)	8 1/2in (21.5cm)	7 1/4in (18.5cm)
110	11in (28cm)	9 1/4in (23.5cm)	8in (20cm)
120	12in (30.5cm)	10in (25.5cm)	8 3/4in (22cm)
130	13in (33cm)	11in (27.5cm)	9 1/2in (24cm)
140	14in (36cm)	11 3/4in (30cm)	10in (25.5cm)
150	15in (38.5cm)	12 1/2in (32cm)	10 3/4in (27.5cm)
160	16in (41cm)	13 1/2in (34cm)	11 1/2in (29cm)
170	17in (43.5cm)	14 1/4in (36cm)	12 1/4in (31cm)
180	18in (46cm)	15in (38.5cm)	13in (33cm)
190	19in (48.5cm)	16in (40.5cm)	13 3/4in (34.5cm)
200	20in (51cm)	16 3/4in (42.5cm)	14 1/2in (36.5cm)
220	22in (56cm)	18 1/2in (47cm)	15 3/4in (40cm)
240	24in (61cm)	20in (51cm)	17 1/4in (44cm)

TABLE 93

chart squares	16hpi	18hpi	20hpi
80	5in (13cm)	4 ½in (11.5cm)	4in (10.5cm)
90	5 ¾in (14.5cm)	5in (13cm)	4 ½in (11.5cm)
100	6 ¼in (16cm)	5 ¾in (14.5cm)	5in (13cm)
110	7in (17.5cm)	6 ¼in (15.5cm)	5 ½in (14cm)
120	7 ½in (19cm)	6 ¾in (17cm)	6in (15.5cm)
130	8 ¼in (21cm)	7 ¼in (18.5cm)	6 ½in (16.5cm)
140	8 ¾in (22.5cm)	8in (20cm)	7in (18cm)
150	9 ½in (24cm)	8 ½in (21.5cm)	7 ½in (19cm)
160	10in (25.5cm)	9in (23cm)	8in (20.5cm)
170	10 ¾in (27cm)	9 ½in (24cm)	8 ½in (22cm)
180	11 ¼in (29cm)	10in (25.5cm)	9in (23cm)
190	12in (30.5cm)	10 ¾in (27cm)	9 ½in (24.5cm)
200	12 ½in (32cm)	11 ¼in (28.5cm)	10in (25.5cm)
220	13 ¾in (35cm)	12 ¼in (31cm)	11in (28cm)
240	15in (38.5cm)	13 ½in (34cm)	12in (30.5cm)

Index